ESCAPE FROM THE TWIN TOWERS

Andra Serlin Abramson
with thanks to
Greg Trevor and Florence Engoran for their stories

CLASH
by ticktock

Copyright © ticktock Entertainment Ltd 2008

First published in Great Britain in 2008 by ticktock Media Ltd,
2 Orchard Business Centre, North Farm Road, Tunbridge Wells, Kent, TN2 3XF

project editor: Ruth Owen
ticktock project designer: Sara Greasley
ticktock picture researcher: Lizzie Knowles

With thanks to series editors Honor Head and Jean Coppendale,
and consultant Mark J. Sachner.

Thank you to Lorraine Petersen and the members of nasen

ISBN 978 1 84696 717 7 pbk

Printed in China

Picture credits (t=top; b=bottom; c=centre; l=left; r=right):
Sean Adair/ Reuters/ Corbis: 16-17. AFP/ Getty Images: 19. age fotostock/ SuperStock: 8-9. Andrea Boohers/ Rex
Features: 27b. Roderick Chen/ SuperStock: 7. Chris Collins/ Corbis: 10, 18. Emmanuel Faure / SuperStock: 4. Erik
Freeland/Corbis: 26. Mike Ford/ SuperStock: 14. Getty Images: 2, 20-21, 24. Ann Giordano/ Corbis: 13. Peter Horree/
Alamy: 5. Rob Howard/ Corbis: OFC. Image Source/ SuperStock: 11t. Jupiter Images: 23. John Labriola/ AP/ PA
Photos: 22. Lisette Le Bon/ SuperStock: 15. Lower Manhattan Development Cop/ Corbis: 31. Heathcliff O'Malley/ Rex
Features: 27t. PhotoAlto / SuperStock : 11b. Reuters/ Corbis: 25, 28, 29. Sipa Press/ Rex Features: 12. Shutterstock:
6 (both). Peter Turnley/Corbis: 1.

Every effort has been made to trace copyright holders, and we apologise in advance for any omissions. We would be
pleased to insert the appropriate acknowledgments in any subsequent edition of this publication.

Contents

CHAPTER 1

JUST ANOTHER DAY

Tuesday, September 11, 2001, was a bright, sunny day. The skies were blue.

In New York, the streets were filled with people.

Children were going to school.
People were heading to work.

The towers of the World Trade Center sparkled in the sunlight.

The World Trade Center was a group of seven office buildings. The two tallest buildings were called the Twin Towers.
The towers stood side-by-side. Each building was 110 storeys high.

Twin Towers

Thousands of people worked in the Twin Towers.

CHAPTER 2

HIJACKED!

 **Three hundred and twenty kilometres from New York, it was a busy morning at Logan International Airport in Boston.**

On the runway, two planes were ready for take-off.

American Airlines Flight 11 and United Airlines Flight 175 were heading for Los Angeles, California.

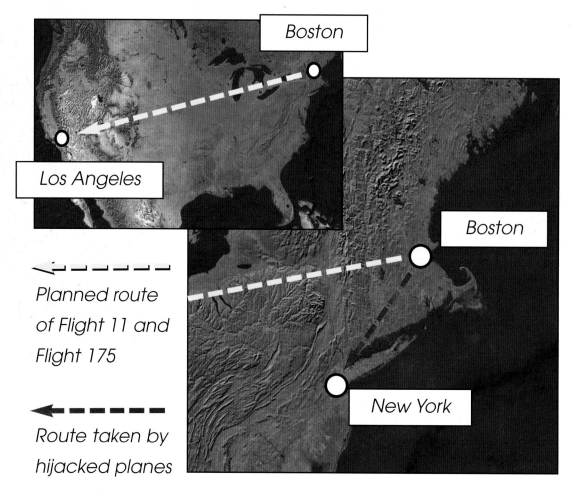

Boston

Los Angeles

Boston

New York

Planned route of Flight 11 and Flight 175

Route taken by hijacked planes

Soon after take-off, Flight 11 was hijacked by terrorists. The hijackers took control of the cockpit. They flew the plane towards New York.

Reconstruction of hijackers in the plane's cockpit

Minutes later, Flight 175 was hijacked. This plane also headed for New York.

08:30

In New York, Greg Trevor was hard at work at the World Trade Center.

Greg was working on the 68th floor of the North Tower.

08:40

Florence Engoran was heading to work.
On the 55th floor of the South Tower,
Florence got out of the lift.
It was a normal day.

But in five minutes, nothing would be the same again!

North Tower

South Tower

CHAPTER 3 THE FIRST IMPACT

 **At 8:46 am, Greg Trevor finished a phone call. He stood up to stretch his legs.**

At that moment, there was a huge crash.
American Airlines Flight 11 slammed into Greg's building.

North Tower

The plane hit the North Tower about 20 floors above Greg's office.

Greg remembers hearing a loud noise.
Then he heard an explosion.

Greg felt the building sway back and forth. He saw glass and paper falling outside his window. He heard alarm bells ringing.

Reconstruction

08 : 50 The air began to fill with smoke.

Greg and the other workers knew they had to leave the building – fast!

The lifts weren't working because of the crash. They started the long walk down hundreds of stairs.

Reconstruction

08:55

North Tower

Outside on the streets and in nearby buildings, people watched in horror.

The North Tower was in flames.
Parts of the building were falling to the ground.
Thick, black smoke was filling the sky.

Across New York, fire alarms and police radios were calling police, firefighters and ambulance crews to the scene.

Within minutes, hundreds of rescue workers were heading to the World Trade Center.

CHAPTER 4

THE SECOND IMPACT

Florence Engoran reached her office on the 55th floor of the South Tower.

Florence didn't see or hear the plane hit the North Tower, but people in her office were talking about it.

Florence and her workmates decided they should start work. But soon, huge bits of concrete and burning papers were falling past Florence's office window.

Reconstruction

"I didn't go back to pick up my bag. I turned right around and ran to the fire steps."

Florence Engoran

On the South Tower stairs, people were scared.

A woman behind Florence screamed,
"Go faster! Go faster!"

Florence screamed back,
"I'm going as fast as I can!"

Reconstruction

By now, the disaster in New York was live on
TV news shows around the world.

09:03

As millions of people around the world watched, United Airlines Flight 175 crashed into the South Tower.

Flight 175

By now, Florence Engoran had reached the 20th floor.

"I held onto the handrail. The impact knocked people over if you didn't hold on. The building moved two to three metres. Everyone stopped dead because the building was swaying so badly."

South Tower

The plane crashed into floors 87 to 93.

CHAPTER 5

INSIDE THE SOUTH TOWER

09:05

**Inside the South Tower
people began to panic.**

**"The lights went out. Concrete and dust started
to fill the stairwell. We were breathing it in.
People started to scream. No one was moving.
I could smell the jet fuel. It smelled like petrol."**
Florence Engoran

09:50 At last, Florence made it down to the first floor. The police were waiting at the bottom of the stairs.

"Run!" The police yelled.

Florence ran as fast as she could.

When she turned around, she was shocked. Both towers were in flames. Pieces of them were falling to the ground.

Florence kept running. She knew she had to get away from the buildings.

09:59

The jet fuel from the planes caused huge fireballs inside the towers. The fire was so hot it made steel columns inside the towers melt.

At 09:59 am, the South Tower collapsed.

Millions of tonnes of steel and concrete crashed down. People in the streets ran for their lives.

CHAPTER 6

INSIDE THE NORTH TOWER

Greg Trevor had been carefully making his way down the stairs of the North Tower.

"I wasn't scared at first," Greg remembers.

Nobody knew the South Tower had collapsed.

Every now and then, the people on the stairs moved over to make way for firefighters. The firefighters were heading up the stairs towards the fire.

Finally, Greg and the other people reached the fourth floor of the North Tower.

Panic! The emergency door was jammed. They were trapped.

The stairs were filled with smoke and concrete dust from the collapsed South Tower. The lights went out. It was hard to breathe. A stream of water ran down the stairs.

"It felt like we were wading through a dark, dirty, fast river – at night, in the middle of a forest fire."
Greg Trevor

10 : 15

For the first time, Greg was afraid he wouldn't make it out alive.

Greg whispered a prayer, **"Lord, please let me see my family again."**

Minutes passed. On the other side of the door, the police were working to open it. Finally the door opened.

A police officer yelled, "Run for the exit!"

Outside the building the air was filled with dust. Greg felt like he was walking through a dirty snowstorm.

10:28

At 10:28 am a rumble drowned out all other sounds.

The North Tower collapsed.

CHAPTER 7

NEW YORK'S SADDEST DAY

10:45

After the buildings collapsed, people stared at the skyline. There was an empty space where the Twin Towers used to be.

People were shocked and dazed.
Strangers joined hands with strangers.
They hugged each other. People cried.

On New York's saddest day, New Yorkers came together.
They helped each other as they never had before.

The towers that were once 110 storeys high were now a twisted mound of metal. Everything inside was crushed into dust. It took days to put out all the fires.

Rescue workers began searching through the rubble. Using machines, dogs and even their bare hands, they searched for survivors. They didn't find many.

For many people, the world changed forever on September 11, 2001.

At the time, no one knew how many people had been killed. All the world knew was that many families had lost loved ones.

At the scene, friends and relatives left photos of missing loved ones hoping someone had seen them.

At least 2,751 people were killed in New York on September 11, 2001. All 147 people on the two planes died. The other victims were the people in the towers and rescue workers.

Police officers, ambulance workers and firefighters rushed to the scene to help. But 412 of them were killed – most when the towers fell. Without their bravery, many more people may have died.

Greg and Florence were two of the survivors.
For them, September 11 will always be a day to remember the people who were not so lucky.

NEED TO KNOW WORDS

collapse To fall down or crumble into pieces.

fireball A very, very hot ball of fire made by an explosion.

hijack To take over and control a plane or vehicle by force.

impact When one thing hits another.

Pentagon A five-sided building that is the headquarters of the United States Department of Defense. The Pentagon is in Arlington, Virginia, USA.

reconstruction An image created to show what happened during an event. Reconstruction images are used in some places in this book. This is because no photographs are available of a particular event or moment in time.

scene The place where an action or event takes place.

skyline The shape of the buildings in a city when seen against the sky.

survivor A person who is still alive after an event or accident in which they might have been killed.

terrorist A person who tries to frighten people or governments into doing what he or she wants by using violence or threatening to use violence.

victim A person who is hurt or killed.

World Trade Center A group of seven office buildings in New York. The World Trade Center included the Twin Towers.

Two other US planes were hijacked on September 11. One plane hit the Pentagon, near Washington, D.C. The other crashed in a field in Pennsylvania. The passengers on this plane tried to take back control from the hijackers. In total, 2,994 people died in the attacks on the US, including 19 terrorists.

The place where the Twin Towers stood is now known as "Ground Zero". A park with a memorial will be built there. The memorial will be called "Reflecting Absence". The names of everyone who died at the World Trade Center will be listed there.

This is a model of the memorial "Reflecting Absence".

READ MORE ONLINE

Websites

http://www.911digitalarchive.org/
The story of everything that happened on September 11

http://www.pbs.org/wgbh/buildingbig/wonder/structure/world_trade.html
Website about the construction and collapse of the World Trade Center Twin Towers